POWER FULL

POWER FULL by Sandy Stream

ISBN: 978-0-9938828-8-3
Hardcover: 978-0-9938828-4-5
eBook:978-0-9938828-9-0

Cover: Galina Spivak
Interior: Barış Şehri *sehribookdesign.com*
Illustration: Galina Spivak
Editors: Elizabeth Zack and Mozelle Jordan

Copyright © 2024 Sandy Stream Publishing.
Montreal, Canada. All rights reserved. No part of this book may be reproduced, distributed, stored in a retrieval system, or transmitted in any form or by any means without the written permission of Sandy Stream Publishing.

thecouragecircle.com

POWER FULL

Sandy Stream

I'm Open

What would I write about if I have absolutely no fear?

Nothing.

What will I write about despite my fear?

This book, about Power.

Why am I afraid? Because I know that some people will not appreciate what I write, and sometimes, when people don't appreciate things, they resort to violence. My fear is normal.

Why will I write this book anyway?

Because I will.

Because I must.

Because I can.

Because I am more powerful than those using Force.

I am more powerful because I know who I am.

I am LOVE.

The intention of this book is to bring to light the Power that we can all live with in harmony and to dispel the myths about Force.

I don't need to explain the difference between
Power and Force since we can *feel* it.

What I will share is the different expressions of Power that I know of, with my deep conviction that if we understood these, there would not be any war, any suffering, or anything to worry about.

This is a big statement.

So, let's see if it's true.

Join me as we explore different expressions of Power, one by one, and see where we end up at the end of this book.

If you'd like to live in Peace and Power, then seize as many of these as you can and hold on to them forever.

They are absolutely yours to keep!

Where Are My Powers?

I am writing this book knowing deeply that every single one of these Powers exists in every moment. So, there's no need to look into the past, the future, or to someone else for them.

Since they are here now, the only thing you need to do is *see* them and *step into* them, just as you would when you hover over a 'superpower' while playing a video game, immediately embodying it. Except in this case, once you have found a Power, no one—and I mean no one—can take it away from you. So, let's start and see how many of these we can find!

And remember, they are all here, right now—for you.

The Power
to Listen

The Power to Listen
is one of our most
beautiful Powers, and
it is ever-present.

You may listen to
music and be moved.

You may listen to a
friend and offer
understanding.

You may listen to
yourself to know what
you need, what to do
next, and to respect
what you hear.

As long as you are
alive, you possess
this ability to listen.

Those who use Force
are attempting to stop
you from listening to
Life and to yourself.

They simply cannot.

This Power is stronger
than Force.

The Power to Breathe

You can breathe
to find your calm,
to let things go,
to inhale energy
from the Earth,
and to make space
in yourself for
the new.

You can breathe
to invite energy in
and to allow
energy out.

Those using Force
try to control your
breath by creating
fear in you.

But as long as you
are alive, you can
choose how to
breathe.

And thus, this
Power wins over
Force, once again.

The Power of Loving Yourself

This Power will guide
you into accepting
yourself as you are,
as you learn, and
as you grow.

It will allow you to
be kind to yourself
when you make
mistakes and compel
you to ask for what
you need.

Those using Force
may try to put you
down, demean,
dismiss, reject, or
disapprove of you.

No matter what they
do, they cannot make
you 'unlove' yourself
or see yourself in the
way they do.

This Power is
unshakable, despite
all external attempts
to rattle it.

The Power of Patience

You have the Power
to wait until it's time.

Plant your seeds and
trust in Life.

Those using Force may
try to convince you that
your seeds won't grow.

This is untrue!

Life will always move
in the way it must, and
no amount of Force
can stop that.

Use your Power to
plant seeds and be
patient.

No one can Force
you to give up
on Life.

The Power of Forgiveness

Forgive yourself
for everything.

Forgive everyone
for everything,
while learning the
lessons that need
to be learned,
and maintaining
your boundaries.

This will free up
tremendous energy!

No one using Force
can stop you from
using your Power
to forgive and from
getting your Life's
energy back.

The Power of the 1%

No matter the amount of
Force anyone in the world
uses, you can look inside
and find some way you
might be supporting the
situation.

This finding is critical,
even if you discover
you are just a 1%
participant in the
situation.

For anything to occur,
it takes a whole 100%.

Removing your part, no
matter how small, will make
the entire thing collapse.

So, understand what you
are feeding, and just STOP.

It takes no energy to stop.

And doing so has the Power
to take apart all dynamics
in which you play a part.

The Power
to Move like a Wave

There is no need to
bounce and collide
with everything in
the world.

Learn to move smoothly
like a wave, like the
sound of music flowing
through the wind and
into your heart.

And when anyone using
Force tries to control
your movement, you can
unleash this wave inside
when the time is right.

Find what is frozen and
allow the movement of
Life to resolve it.

Movement cannot be
stopped by Force. It is
always going to 'win',
since Life is infinite
movement.

The Power
to Unlearn

By focusing on the Truth, no matter how painful it is, you can always unlearn anything that was Forced upon you during your younger years.

Your ability to unlearn is far more powerful than anyone's attempt to Force ideas, since unlearning has the Truth on its side.

And the Truth can always be *felt*, no matter what you have been taught.

By using your Power to question everything and by being continuously open to unlearning, no one can ever permanently ingrain anything into you.

The Power to Create

Every moment is a moment
of creation, either by
destroying falsehood or
by creating the new.

Do not be afraid to create,
as it is your essence!

The Power of Creation, in
its infinite ways, can never
be controlled by Force.

No matter the circumstance
in which we individually or
collectively find ourselves,
we can always create.

It is the most natural human
activity once we have been
liberated from our self-
imposed limits.

The Power to Express

There are times when we
find ourselves called to
express ourselves with
courage and inner fire.

This kind of expression
is done without any
'against-ness' and is
deeply personal.

It can be in a painting, in
music, or in a cartoon.

It can be in spoken or
written words—in a
poem, a courageous
expression of boundaries,
or a warm hello.

It can be through
movement—a dance,
tending a garden, or
the powerful act
of walking away.

It can be a silent
invitation, sitting
in peaceful stillness.

It can be in any form.

And while we are in this courageous state of Pure Expression, we are not preoccupied with repercussions.

There is no attempt to control the results that may ensue.

This is not the same kind of expression as Forceful Expression.

Though it is often loud, Forceful Expression has no power whatsoever, because it is based on fear and falsehood; it simply has nothing behind it.

Life is constantly moving
us toward a state of
individual Pure Expression.

Infused in Pure Expression
is the Universe and Life,
which is above, below,
and completely *with* such
expression.

And when we are carried
into expressing ourselves in
this state, Life will take care
of *everything* that needs to be
taken care of in connection
with it.

Pure Expression can move
mountains without any Force
since it is fully and completely
supported by Life.

I am LOVE

I can move everything

without any Force.

Afterword

This is not my book.

The ideas come from wherever they come, and I write them down as truthfully as I can as I decipher them.

I am the reader of this book, and all my books, constantly trying to understand what is written.

One thing I know for sure is that the hardest thing for me has been to look in the mirror. And as I read this book, I know that I must take an honest look to see if, and when, I am using Force. It would be too easy to think the book is talking about "other people" when it mentions those who use Force.

To live in Power, we need to remove ourselves from the Force and control system by noticing when we criticize or try to control others and Life itself. We also need to check whether there is any inner Force at play, including controlling, criticizing, and beating ourselves up, which we can unlearn (see the Power to Unlearn).

I hope this book was useful to you, and I wish you courage on your journey.

Is there any other way to truly live?

Sandy Stream

thecouragecircle.com

www.ingramcontent.com/pod-product-compliance
Lightning Source LLC
Chambersburg PA
CBHW051607010526
44119CB00056B/811